THE QUITTER'S GUIDE TO FINISHING

THE QUITTER'S GUIDE TO FINISHING
101 Ways to Get Where You Want to Be

Betsy Schow

THE COUNTRYMAN PRESS
A division of W. W. Norton & Company
Independent Publishers Since 1923

For information about permission to reproduce selections
from this book, write to Permissions, The Countryman Press,
500 Fifth Avenue, New York, NY 10110

For information about special discounts for bulk
purchases, please contact W. W. Norton Special Sales
at specialsales@wwnorton.com or 800-233-4830

Manufacturing by Versa Press
Book design by Anna Reich
Production manager: Devon Zahn

The Countryman Press
www.countrymanpress.com

A division of W. W. Norton & Company
500 Fifth Avenue, New York, NY 10110
www.wwnorton.com

978-1-68268-015-5

10 9 8 7 6 5 4 3 2 1

For my husband, who lets me share our lives and
my spaz outs with the masses.

CONTENTS

INTRODUCTION

Hello, my name is Betsy. And I am a recovering Quitter.

(Hi, Betsy)

If this strikes you as the beginning of some support meeting, like Quitter's Anonymous, you're not too far off.

For most of my life, I was that kid. The one the teachers always harassed for not living up to their potential. In fact, the only thing I truly excelled at was quitting. You name it—I've probably attempted and quit it at some point. I'd get these grand ideas of how to make my life better. I'd get excited about this diet or that workout routine. Or try starting a new hobby or project. On multiple occasions that included attempting to write a book. That was all well and good, but unfortunately, within a few weeks, the excitement would fade and that little voice would kick in. You know the one I'm talking about: "You're no good at this. You'll never keep the weight off. Why are you even bothering?" That little voice kept me from finishing . . . anything.

So after many years of being fat and miserable, with a few years mixed in of being average and less miserable, I finally had a lightbulb moment. The reason I was unhappy was not the extra 75 pounds around my middle. Rather, it was the weight of all the things unfinished that pulled me down, making it impossible to move forward.

You see, every time I'd get a new idea and quit, each one of those abandoned goals became a stone that piled at my feet. Then my mountain of failures would get a little higher, making success that much harder to see or reach.

The adventure that changed me from Quitter to Finisher started the day I broke the scale and had yet another one of those grand plans to lose weight. Except this time, by complete accident, it went beyond the pounds and snowballed into a year of changing my life and accomplishing seemingly impossible dreams. One of those dreams was to write a book and share my experiences with others. With a lot of hard work and help, my first book, *Finished Being Fat*, came to life on the page.

Now, one of things I've heard at book signings or speaking to people about my book is, "What does 'Finished Being Fat' even mean? Just because you're skinnier now, you can say that? That's a pretty bold statement."

The answer is always that my new and improved life has less to do with the shift in number on the scale and more to do with the shift in my state of mind.

I was fat. Huge. Ginormous. Not because of the number embroidered on the tag of my jeans, but because of all those failures I carried around with me every day. My low self-esteem and depression very nearly destroyed my family. Obesity is an epidemic, but so is this unquenchable drive to be better, thinner than the woman standing next to us. Even if that woman is us, looking back from the mirror. I couldn't see past my own judgments for fear that someone else's would be even worse.

The concepts behind *Finished Being Fat* are much more than preoccupations with outside appearances. How many people worry that they aren't successful because they are a stay-at-home mom instead of a business professional? How many people devalue themselves as a person of worth because they feel that they are not enough? That they are broken and not worth loving? Those worries and self-doubts can wriggle deep within our souls and infect every part of our existence with feelings of failure.

And that's why I wrote *Finished Being Fat*. It's my story, my quest to change the way I looked at my life and myself. It's about how everything became different once I learned the Philosophy of Finishing, and could give that girl in the mirror a hug and say, "I love you at any size, and you can be anything you want to be." What I want for everyone—male or female, fit or fat—is to discover the Philosophy of Finishing and change the way they see themselves and their lives. To gain the tools and the self-confidence to make goals, tackle the impossible, and find success and peace within their lives.

Because it's not about the fat or failure—it's about the finish.

Finishing changed my life. It continues to change my life. Using the Philosophy of Finishing, I am not only a happier and healthier person, I'm finally completing all those grand ideas. For me, I know I can finish anything and everything I set out to do.

I am a finisher.

My life is a success.

And everyone else can have the same thing.

During my yearlong adventure, I climbed a real mountain that darn near killed me, but the one I'm going to guide you up is not built of granite, but of the stones and challenges that are unique to you. Your goal is at the summit, and like a Sherpa, I want to show you the way there by sharing some of my favorite quotes, personal sayings, stories, and some meditations/exercises I use when goal keeping that are universal to any goal, whether you want to lose weight, run a marathon, organize your house, finish school, get a better career, be smoke-free, or finally get going on your quest for world domination.

You don't need expensive equipment, coaching, or seminars. All you need is a willingness to look at things through a new lens. These 101 little tweaks in your brain will lead to a course correction in your life and let you tackle any mountain before you. Are you ready to take that first step?

STEP ONE:

Choose Your Mountain

(Beware of the Ones with
Sharp, Pointy Spikes)

T HE FIRST STEP IS ALWAYS A DOOZY. Aside from admitting that you have a quitting problem, you have to decide how to go about correcting that. Which mountain do you need to climb? What matters to you? What has been weighing you down?

Not all mountains are the same height. And it makes little sense to climb Everest if you'd keel over hiking to the house at the top of the hill. What you choose as a goal—how you word and look at that goal—sets the tone that can carry you through to the summit.

This section will help you psych up and identify which mountain is the one you need to take on right now and help you avoid the ones with the impassable cliffs.

#1

Philosophy of Finishing

Not everyone can win the race, but everyone can finish it.

Start off with the right mind-set—you aren't striving to come in first. Or to beat or outdo anyone else. This is not a game or race to quit midway through if it's not going well, or if you make a mistake. The entire purpose is only to keep on the path. Finish no matter how long it takes or what you have to go through.

Your first action along the path is to write in the space provided, "I am a finisher. I promise I will cross the finish line no matter what."

There. You've just made a commitment to yourself. The journey has started—now on to seeing it through.

#2

An ideal is a dangerous lie. A mirage of hope as you cross a desert, which blocks out everything else from sight. As you get closer, that cool sparkling water continues to be just out of reach, no matter how far you travel. Eventually you turn back defeated or keep going and die of thirst. Ideals are impossible to achieve, because they don't exist in reality.

It's a trap.

Don't fall for it.

An ideal is a false finish line. Completely unattainable, even with the best genetics and all the luck in the world. It's the quest to be "Enough" to fill that hole in your soul. Everybody falls in this snake pit sometimes, prey to the venom within it.

I'll be happy when I'm _____ enough.

Smart
Pretty
Thin
Rich
Organized
Good

Here's a secret: It's never enough because you're filling a bucket that still has a leak in the bottom. So right now, remove the word "enough" from your vocabulary.

#3

There are countless mountains to climb and countless goals you could try to achieve. So how do you settle for just one?

I suggest a mind map or table to plot out what you need in your life.

Refer to the writing space on the next page. Separate it into four columns:

> Personal/Spiritual
> Family/Home
> Career/Money
> Physical/Health

These are four very generalized areas of a person's life. In each column, start writing out things that you feel you'd be happier with. Here are some common examples:

Personal/Spiritual	Family/Home	Career/Money	Physical/Health
Would be happier if I had more time to myself	Family togetherness time	More $$$	Lose weight
Better relationship with spouse	House clean enough for company	Higher position	Stop smoking
Travel more		Get out of debt	Eat healthy
		Learn a new skill	
		Get college degree	

Now start prioritizing them. What is nice to have versus what you need in order to get through another year. Also think about what could cross over multiple categories. If I lost weight, would my relationship be better? Is that something we could do as a family? Which of these needs are you most passionate about working on?

Bookmark this page. Think about what sorts of actions you might take to fulfill these needs until a few pages later when I have you refer back to this.

Personal/Spiritual	Family/Home	Career/Money	Physical/Health

#4

Happiness is not something that happens to you. It's something you make happen.

#5

Goal. Dream. Many people swap around these words as if they were synonymous. Guess what? They're not.

I could wax poetic for pages and invoke every Disney fairy tale you've ever seen, but I will keep it simple and practical. To the point.

A goal is a defined finish line that your actions can lead you to. A dream is a subjective outcome that you can't fully control.

Here's a set of examples:

1. I'm going to finish a marathon this year.
2. I'm going to finish a marathon in first place this year.

The first example is a goal. Something with a deadline that is absolutely achievable with training and dedication. Meeting that goal relies primarily on the effort put forth. The second example is a dream. If you do all the things required, train hard and to the best of your ability, getting first place still depends on how fast other people are. That is outside of your control.

Dreams are important to strive for, but whether you achieve them does not make you a success. Setting goals and taking all the actions in your control to achieve them and crossing that finish line . . . that's success. No matter if you came in first place or last.

#6

I don't care if you are 15 or 50—it's never too late to change and strive for a new goal, as long as your heart is still beating. And even then, I'm pretty sure God or a really good heart surgeon can make exceptions.

We are ever changing, ever adapting. I will never be the same today as I was yesterday. And tomorrow I will be different as well. Accept that the past can't be changed and commit to reaching forward to what you want your future to be.

#7

Life is a journey and you have three choices on how you travel through it:

1. Plop yourself in the driver's seat and steer where you want to go.
2. Hitchhike and catch a ride. Wait to see where you end up.
3. Stay still and end up roadkill.

#8

Don't be tofu.

Seriously. Tofu is great in stir fry and curry, but it sucks as a personality. Let me explain. By itself, tofu is neutral. Bland. No real taste of its own. However, tofu is a sponge and absorbs all the other flavors around it. Which is fine for a food-like substance, but poses great problems when selecting a goal. If you try to follow someone else's path, borrow their dream without a burning desire of your own, then you are the equivalent of tofu—soaking up the flavor of those around you. Find your own unique flavor and go after it.

#9

Active Goals Using the 3 Ws

How you phrase your goal is very important. It's setting up your finish line. It's detailing your expectations and conditions for success. It's differentiating what is a dream from what is in your control. The goals are based on actions that you control.

Alright, remember #3, where you plotted out a mind map or table on what you felt you needed in life?

Pull that table back out. Consider the area that most drew your attention, where you felt the most drive to change. Highlight it and write it in the space on the next page.

For the sake of demonstration, I'm going to pretend that mine was a three-way tie.

FEEL BETTER ABOUT MYSELF
BE HEALTHIER
LOSE WEIGHT

Now these three things may be imperative to giving me a better life, but as goals they kinda suck. They are way too broad. I can't reach the finish line if I can't see that waving checkered flag. Otherwise I could just keep going forever. If I moosh together these three things, I get the idea that if I lead a healthier lifestyle, then chances are I will lose weight and feel better about myself.

Now as I add details to the goal, I want to be very careful to keep it within my control. I could say, "I want to lose 20 pounds in three months' time." Well, what if I exercise and eat well, but the genetics or hormones of my body say . . . nope. And, although

I did everything in my power, I only lose 14 pounds. What should be a success ends up feeling like a failure. So instead, think of the weight loss as a lovely trophy, but not the finish line.

I've found the best goal statements include the 3 Ws. Who, What, and When. The Who is easy: You. The What and When focus on an action and deadline. So I would take that "Be healthier" and detail out a measurable goal of my needs and the timeframe I want to commit to making it happen.

Which action helps you get there will depend on your goal. For this one I would expand it to something like this:

In six months, I will be healthier, have more energy, and my clothes will fit better because I am going to exercise 3 to 5 times a week and eat more whole foods and less added sugar.

And just like that, you have a goal to be healthier, and an action you are promising to take to get you there. In the next step, you will take that action goal into an action plan. But as you go through the rest of the book, keep your goal firmly in your mind.

#10

Goals are not one size fits all. What matters is that the goal fits you. Don't think you need to climb Everest just because it's the tallest and it's there. Instead find your Everest—the challenge that will prove you can do anything you set your mind to.

Everything is impossible until someone has the guts to prove it can be done.

#12

You don't have to be great to start, but you have to start to be great.
—Zig Ziglar

There's something all of us humans have in common—we are all born little squiggly naked things, dependent on other people. You have to start at square one and grow. Goals are pretty much the same concept. If you were already awesome at something, it wouldn't be much of a goal, would it?

#13

A big bumblebee shouldn't be able to fly. Its wings are too small and fragile to lift up that big fat body. Luckily for the flowers and honey lovers of the world, no one bothered to tell the bee—or if they did, the bee ignored them and kept flying anyway.

#14

Dreams can change the direction of your thoughts, but *Goals* can change the direction of your life.

#15

Starter's High

Ready. Set. Go.

Even hearing those words, my chest tightens as endorphins and adrenaline course through my system. A new beginning. A new hope. The new possibility that just maybe this time I won't suck.

I call that feeling the starter's high. That rush, the biological pick-me-up that gets me so excited about whatever project I'm about to begin. It's addicting, and without care can be dangerous.

Before I learned how to finish, my life had a constant nagging sense of emptiness—more than the black hole I swore lived inside my stomach. Not only did I try filling the void with food, but also with new projects. I would begin a new craft, hobby, goal, or weight loss attempt and the excitement would give me a high, lifting me out of the dumps. For a while at least. But inevitably, the highs faded when reality and 100 pounds of craft supplies came crashing down on me.

Chasing the starter's high led me to seek my next fix, abandoning whatever current project I was on. I would quit and start something new just to perk up. Except those half-finished projects added up—more than just my credit card bill from all the scheming. The quitting dug that hole inside me deeper, and served as a reminder that I was a constant failure.

The starter's high is a drug—used properly, it can motivate you to find your purpose and kick-start you into action. But never forget, it's a crutch. The real reward and rush awaits you at the finish line. And those effects last a heck of a lot longer.

Plot the Course

(Without an Escape Route)

To GET TO YOUR DESTINATION, you need a map or GPS to keep you from turning down the wrong side roads. Similarly, to reach a goal, you've got to have a plan. Only too often we build in a trap door, a way out for when the excitement wears off and things stop looking good. How can we succeed when a part of ourselves already believes we are going to fail?

Use this section to see the trail in front of you and identify the pitfalls. Then plan your route to avoid the worst traps and pack your bag with the right gear to help you get through the rest of the trip.

A goal without a plan to see it through is just wishful thinking.

#17

The Quitter's Dilemma

I've already owned up that I was a charter member of QA (Quitter's Anonymous), addicted to that starter's high. For the first thirty years of my life, I was stuck in the cycle of what I call The Quitter's Dilemma. I'd make those starts, get that rush, and work toward those goals but still be unhappy. So I'd quit.

That's because those past failures never left, and they hung around my neck, weighing me down and keeping me from seeing any possible success. With each start, the effect of the high became shorter and more elusive. Even as I looked forward to whatever new goal I was attempting, those past failures became a constant reminder, proof that I'd never actually succeed since I had tried and failed so many times before. Planning was a joke, since most of my plan was how to explain to everyone when my big grand dream didn't work out. Finally, I decided, why bother trying?

It took the events from my first book, *Finished Being Fat*, to realize that quitting is more than just giving up and moving on to the next project. Quitting builds a wall that is difficult or impossible to see over, leading to a habit of giving up every time we hit that barrier.

So how do you get over a wall?

Build a mountain of finishes.

#18

A goal is merely a finish line, the summit of a mountain. The end point is the same whether you take a helicopter to the peak or get there using your own two feet. The difference is that for one, it was a beautiful flight. For the other, the person who struggles and fights for each step, the view from the top is life changing.

#19

Quitters search for the exit when Plan A falls through.

Finishers search for the ladder back up and try the next plan because they know there are 25 other letters of the alphabet.

#20

Throw Out Your Fat Clothes

I used to believe that things would happen the way they were supposed to. So, I had a place I wanted to end up and a vague idea of how I'd get there. But I never wrote out a plan, because if it was meant to be, it would be.

Which of course is an excuse and a blatant load of crap to avoid responsibility when things would go awry like they always seemed to.

What I eventually noticed was that while I didn't have a plan of how to succeed, I always seemed to have a detailed backup plan or graceful exit for when I failed. My husband pointed this out to me when we were cleaning the garage in the middle of my weight loss journey. I'd gone from a size 22 to a size 6, so as you can imagine, I shed a fair amount of clothes along with the pounds. After consulting with my dad, a fellow yo-yo dieter, I decided to box up all my fat clothes and store them. Just in case.

I applauded myself for being so smart and frugal. My husband bemoaned both the space it took up in the garage and the space the fear of gaining back the weight took up in my mind. I argued it this way: "How could you want me to throw them out. You were a Boy Scout—wasn't your motto to always be prepared? It's foolish to not protect myself in case something goes wrong. Pre-nups exist for a reason, in case a marriage doesn't work out. If my weight loss turns out like it usually does, then I'll be glad to be prepared."

My husband said it was my choice, but left me with a thought along these lines: "If you spent as much energy planning to stay fit as you do worrying about getting fat again, you wouldn't need a safety net. And our garage wouldn't be so cluttered."

He was right of course. And it was something I did subconsciously. Like making sure I knew the withdrawal and refund policies when I started a community college class. Just in case life happened.

I should have been making life happen, but I spent so much time and energy waiting for it to crash down on me instead. And I won't lie, sometimes it does. Still, plan like success is the only option and find a way to deal with whatever comes at you. Otherwise, making a bail-out plan just means you have one foot stuck in the exit and it's hard to climb a mountain with one foot.

#21

I'd rather attempt to do something great and fail, than to attempt nothing and succeed.   *—Robert H. Schuller*

Trying is hard. And scary. Writing out the details of the plan—and realizing what I am actually in for—still causes me panic attacks on occasion. Can I really do this? Will it really make things better?

The answer is yes, because every step is still an inch farther than if you stood still.

A plan is not just words on paper.
It's a call to action.
A promise you make to yourself that you'll follow through in order make your life better. Because you deserve it.

#23

The Why

Sometimes the difference between a quitter and a finisher is a simple Why. As in "Why the hell am I doing this?" Your Why has to stand up and do battle with all the Why Nots when things get hard. And I warn you, whether you want to lose weight, get a degree, run a race, clean your house, or break a habit, you need a pretty strong Why because the Why Nots are legion.

> "I'm too old."
> "It's too expensive."
> "I just don't have the time."
> "People don't support what I'm doing."
> "I can slack off just this once."
> "This is harder than I thought."

Your Why Nots may be different but they all lead down the same easy path . . . to quitting.

From personal experience, I can tell you it's a lot better and easier to find your Why at the start than in the middle of your adventure. Because if you are like me, it's a whole heck of a lot harder to find motivation at Oh-God-Why in the morning when your alarm goes off and you'd much rather curl back under the covers than go jogging. When this happened to me, my Why needed to be tough enough to convince me that it was still worth going forward, even while knowing I'd be sore and tired and would freeze my butt off.

So before you start climbing your personal Everest or striving for your goal, look deep and find your Why.

#24

Finding Your Why

Time to flip back to that trusty table of things we worked on in Choose Your Mountain #3 (page 5). Look at what you said you needed in your life, the one that led you to your action goal. Why do you need that thing?

Whatever you are thinking, dig deeper. If the thought doesn't make you tear up a little, or illicit strong emotion, it won't be enough to get you through to the end.

My very common example, you will recall, was to feel better about myself, be healthy, and lose weight. If the only reason I want to lose weight is so I can fit into some frilly dress . . . guess what? I'm going to find a cuter dress in a bigger size as soon as the next craving for cheesecake hits.

I will share my Why. What gets my butt up to jog or walk around my lake nearly every day? It's my girls. Being healthy makes me a better mother. It makes me happier. It makes me like myself more when I look in the mirror. I want to be the sort of example that my girls can learn from. I don't want them to grow up like I did—bawling and despising myself anytime I had to undress in front of a mirror. I want to show them what body positivity is at any shape. That feeling good and being happy is beautiful—not those dumb photoshopped pictures.

Maybe you want to be healthy so you can be around in twenty years for your grandkids. Maybe you need a light and a win in your life just to survive the next year.

Who's around you? How will their life improve when you reach this goal and become a better person?

What about the person staring back at you in the mirror? What do you owe yourself?

Why do you need this change?

When you find it . . . and your chest tightens and the goosebumps rise to your skin . . . write it down right here.

_____

_____

_____

_____

Now do it again on a separate piece of paper. Write it big. Write it on whatever you can. Post it visibly.

This is the survival kit for your journey—for what will give you light in dark places.

The Why is the reason you're on this journey. The passion behind the Why is fuel that keeps your motor running.

#26

When your Why
is strong, the
How gets easier
to slog through.

If you always fly
by the seat of
your pants . . .
your butt will
soon get awfully
heavy.

#28

Overnight success is a big, fat urban myth. Sure, sometimes it can be your lucky day and you catch lightning in a bottle. But think of it this way: If you didn't have the bottle ready, you would have just been hit by lightning.

#29

The Devil in the Details

A good goal statement had the Who, What, and When. A plan has the Where, Why, and How.

First, take the action goal statement you set in Choose the Mountain #9 (page 13) and write it down. Then, below it add your Why from Plot the Course #24 (page 33).

Let's go to the How. Goals go off track when life intervenes and we don't know how to deal with the unexpected. So take the actions from your goal statement and try to map out all the little hiccups in your life that could keep you from following through.

In my mock statement, I committed to exercise three to five times a week and eat more whole foods. Well, how am I going to do that? What are the obstacles in my way? Do I need to find the time? Do I need to find a clear space? Am I going to force my family to eat the same things I am? Do I know what whole foods are and does a whole cheesecake count?

After you've written out as many questions as you can think of in the writing space provided, answer them one by one on how you will deal with them. If you are out, how do you plan on eating and decide what is acceptable behavior NOW before the smells of butter and sugar hit your nose? Decide how you plan on exercising NOW before you realize that spin class is hard and makes you really sore and oh golly 5 a.m. is early but you promised to volunteer in Jimmy's class later, so that's the only time you have.

Once you've exhausted all your Hows and committed to

going to plan Z if need be, the last piece is the Where. Where will you strive for this goal? Is it going to be in a public forum—are you going to announce it on Facebook? Or is this something you are keeping to yourself? Each has merits, because let's face it— some people are awesome and some are morons about lifestyle changes. I personally believe in a bit of positive peer pressure, which works for me. There are a few other key Wheres.

> Where can you go for support?
> Where can you go for the tough love?
> Where is your goal central? In other words, where
>   do most of the actions happen?
> Where are your safe zones, stress-free places to
>   escape to?
> Where are the war zones with triggers that will lead
>   you astray?

By identifying these as well as you can now, you are putting up Danger, Rock Fall Ahead signs on your mountain as well as marking the first aid tent.

From here, work the plan that you set. Follow through on your Hows. Do the actions. And while you go through the actions, the next sections will help you change the way you think and see those actions.

Point Your Compass Up

(Otherwise Known as Getting Your Inner Critic to Pipe Down)

MORE OFTEN THAN NOT, the person who stands in the way of finishing is the one who stares back in the mirror. In the rear corner of your mind, there's that little voice, the demon, who says "I can't—it's impossible. I'm not good enough." You aren't alone. Everyone has that cruel doubting critic. Everyone has struggled with that negative self-narrative. You, me, even that one lady that everyone hates because she's always on time and sends her kids to school looking like they stepped out of a catalog. That voice exists in us all because we are human.

To be a finisher, you need to change the direction of the conversation in your own head. Reinforce the positive angel voice until it grows loud enough to drown out the devil on your shoulder.

Failure
(fail·ure) ˈfālyər/

Failure does not mean falling short of success, but rather, failure is falling victim to the fear that keeps you from trying again.

#31

66

Nothing can stop the man with the right mental attitude from achieving his goal; nothing on earth can help the man with the wrong mental attitude.

99

—Thomas Jefferson

#32

Brain Budgeting

Negative thoughts are expensive. They waste your time and energy. There's a punitive cost too. Every time negative thoughts dragged me down to quit, I wasted registration fees and materials for projects—and that says nothing for the cost of therapy. Here's an exercise to see just how much your negativity is costing you.

You've heard of a curse word jar. Make a crap jar. Every time you tell yourself some manner of negative crap—I'm fat. I can't. I'm not good enough . . . or if you compare yourself to another—put money in the jar. A quarter. A buck. Even a penny. Do that for a week. Be honest and do it faithfully. Then dump that jar out and really see just how much you are weighing yourself down.

#33

Promise me you'll always remember: You're braver than you believe, and stronger than you seem, and smarter than you think.
—A. A. Milne

My entire life I have struggled with depression and perfectionism. Even as a kid, the world was in black and white. Them and me. The kids who were pretty, thin, and popular. And me, the awkward, chunky girl with an eye patch. When I wasn't being ignored, I was being bullied. Their taunts echoed in my ears and, even before I left elementary school, I remember having the constant and pervasive thought, "I'm not good enough."

That mentality carried on through the years into adulthood. The roller coaster of yo-yo dieting, failed New Year's resolutions, unfinished college degree—all those things piled together and told me one thing only: I was worthless. If I wasn't exactly what I pictured in my mind—the thinnest, best, brightest—well, then I was nothing. As an adult, without a doubt, I was my own harshest critic. Even now, it's something I struggle with. Some days the weight of something I'm not doing well is greater than all the things I've accomplished.

Years ago, I was watching a Winnie the Pooh movie with my kiddos. Winnie the Pooh was afraid he wasn't up to the task of doing something. He feared he wasn't good enough. His faithful pal Christopher Robin said, "Promise me you'll always remember: You're braver than you believe, and stronger than you seem, and smarter than you think." From that point on, whenever Pooh Bear struggled, he remembered those words of his biggest supporter. I muttered out loud, "Gosh, I wish I had someone to say that to me." My little girl climbed onto my lap, squished my cheeks between her palms, and touched her nose to mine.

"Momma should always 'member—you're braver than you leave, stronger than you see, and smarter than you stink."

I laughed hard enough that my eyes leaked. That's my story and I'm sticking to it. Because surely a grown, nearly middle-age woman wouldn't cry over a misquoted Winnie the Pooh line. But ever since then, I have used those words as a mantra. The original quote, that is. I put it on the wall over my desk so I can read it when that feeling of being not good enough creeps in. Whenever I underestimate myself, I just look up and remember that I am braver than I believe, stronger than I seem, and smarter than I think.

#34

Liar, Liar

From even as early as 9 years old, I can clearly recall my inner critic whispering spiteful and discouraging thoughts. It was the bully that fought me at every turn, urging me to give up. It grew louder and crueler each time I quit. There was only one way to truly fight back—I would have to prove the voice wrong and keep going. When I was true to my word, followed through, and reached my goals, I exposed that voice for the liar that it always was. Then that bully no longer had power because every time it piped up, I'd counter back that I had proof that I could finish. I could look at all the things I'd done, what I'd followed through on, and make that voice shrink back to the dark corner from which it came.

Perception is reality. Change your perception, change your reality.

#36

The secret ingredients to being a finisher aren't something that can be bought on a shelf. It's not a diet to be followed, nor a pill to be taken.

It's time and hard work.

But most important, it's coming to the realization that you are worth every moment.

#37

Stained-Glass Windows

There have been days when I've struggled with a depression that pulled me down and weighed my limbs so much that it was difficult to get out of bed. I would get up and do the best I could, but there was that niggling thought that something was wrong with me. I felt broken. Like God made a mistake, and that He should have some return policy for defective merchandise.

Once I shared these feelings with my husband, and he promptly chastised me. How dare I say such a thing about myself! If I felt defective and unworthy, what sort of example was I going to set for our kids? In particular, our daughter who is on the autism spectrum. Was she defective? Less worthy of love than our neuro-normal daughter?

Looking at it that way changed my perspective and the reality of how I deal with my depression. Our special needs daughter was 4 at the time. Now she's 9 and very aware that she is different from other children. My heart breaks when she comes to me crying, asking, "Why am I not like the other kids? I am broken, can't you fix me?"

Every time I reassure her with something based off of what a friend said to me, it also serves as my reminder. Because even though I know better, there are still times when I feel the same as my daughter. This is what I tell her:

"Humans are fragile things, easily broken. When my soul faces constant battering, it feels like I crack and shatter into a thousand pieces like glass. Instead of seeing myself as a jagged heap that will never be whole again, I think of myself as a stained-glass window where every piece comes together to make a mosaic masterpiece."

We need to stop seeing ourselves as rubbish, shards to be swept up and discarded. Instead, we are a work in progress, and each little piece is needed to make our life a unique and beautiful masterpiece.

To gain anything
of value, you
need to believe
you are worth
having it.

You can be
your best friend
or your worst
enemy. The
choice is yours.

#40

Frenemy

Picture that you're out with your best friend. She is having a bit of a rough time, so you turn to her and say:

"You're pathetic. I swear, why do you even bother? It was obvious to me and everyone else that you'd fall flat on your face. Honestly it's embarrassing. You should really give up. Oh, and you're getting really chunky, so you should do something about that."

In this scenario, your friend would smack you and dump a pitcher of water on your head. And rightfully so. No sane person would be so awful to his or her friend or someone they cared about. It's unacceptable, right? Yet, how often have you said similar things to yourself? I know I have. And worse.

Decide right now that you deserve the same respect you would give to your best friend. The second you start to insult yourself, feel that ice dumped on your head and stop.

Negative thoughts are like poison.

Even a small drop spreads and saps your strength. Those drops add up to crippling and even lethal amounts.

   Positive thoughts are the antidote. Administer a healthy dose daily to counter the poison's side effects.

#42

Just Breathe

I will be honest—when I started practicing positive affirmations, the only thing I was positive about was that I felt like a moron. But after I got over my self-consciousness, I felt lighter with each practice. Five years after I started, this one is my favorite and it's given me some of the best nights' sleep of my life.

When you are ready to go to bed, turn off the lights and lay flat on your back.

Place your hands on your chest. Empty your thoughts and focus only on your breathing.

Inhale and count to two. Hold your breath for one count, then exhale one-two-three.

When you have the rhythm down, trade the counts for words.

Inhale, focused on the words "I am." Then hold your breath for a beat and exhale, focusing on the words "capable of anything."

Repeat this again, inhaling to "I am" but on the exhale change the words to whatever you need to hear. "Strong and loved." "A great mother." "Better today than yesterday." It's up to you.

After five of those, change the inhale to "I will be," and then your exhale should be focused on what you need to become. "A finisher." "Able to conquer my fears." "Able to go the distance."

Use the space below to write out your favorites.

_____

_____

_____

_____

Many nights I fall asleep halfway through because my mind is so at peace. In the middle of a hard day, I find a quiet spot and do this sitting exercise in a chair to re-center my thinking. It always helps, and I've only fallen asleep once.

#43

It sucks hanging around people you don't like. And face it—no matter where you go, you can never escape yourself. So since you're stuck with you anyway, save yourself the trouble and just like yourself already.

Forgive yourself for every wrong turn you think you've ever taken.

Because those side trips have led you to this place and this moment. Which is exactly where you needed to be in order to get to the place you need to go.

Bad News: You're not perfect.

Good News: Nobody else is either.

Not even that neighbor who posts to Pinterest every day with all the crafts and dinners she makes. You can't see behind the pictures. I assure you that there has to be some very deep-seeded issues to make someone spend hours learning to fold napkins into the shapes of animals. Be grateful for the imperfections that make you unique, one of a kind, and priceless.

#46

Take a Picture—It'll Last Longer

This is a mindfulness exercise I came up with to combat my negative self-image and train myself to focus on the bigger picture. Let me just preface this by saying that I dislike having my picture taken. As in I despise it with a level of hatred that should be reserved for telemarketers, taxes, and swimsuit shopping. So it's not a surprise that I avoided the camera like it was trying to steal my soul. Because in a way it was. My whole self-image was tainted by fat goggles—like beer goggles, but instead everything around me centers on an obsession with being fat. Whether I was looking at wedding photos, family vacations, or the images I'd get tagged in on Facebook, I could not view the picture without a wince. Inevitably followed by an immediate inner tirade of every single thing I could find wrong with myself in that particular shot. I was too fixated on hating my unfortunate double chin that I completely lost sight of the emotion the moment was intended to capture. I had to retrain my brain to focus positively on the things that mattered.

And here's how you start:

Find a picture. Preferably from an event or trip, to start with.

Take 30 seconds to really study the picture. Then put it away.

Now, using the space provided, for 1 minute write down everything POSITIVE you can remember about the picture. Who else is in the picture? What are they doing? Where was the photo taken? What's a memory from this particular moment?

_____

_____

_____

_____

_____

_____

_____

Time's up. Give yourself a point for each line you wrote down that was not negative. How many could you come up with? Was it hard to shut out critical thoughts of yourself?

Tomorrow, do it again, with a picture from a different place and time in your life. See if it gets easier and if your score improves.

The first time I did this I cried. I could only think of all the things wrong with me. I started doing this regularly, and eventually I got better at it and could recall all my memories of that moment without defaulting first to judgment of myself or the people around me.

STEP FOUR:

Keep a Steady Pace

(So You Don't Faceplant)

WELCOME TO LIMBO, where the initial high from finishing has faded, yet the end of your goal summit is still just a dot on the horizon. It's so easy to procrastinate and turn back when the results are hidden and harder to find than Waldo in a candy cane factory. The secret to avoid getting stuck in the muddy middle is to finish something every day. Forget the starter's high and focus on the feeling and rush from finishing. Because on the way to the big peak, there are lots of smaller ascents. Mini summits to be celebrated that keep self-esteem high so that we feel the accomplishment and the motivation to continue toward those goals.

In this section, focus on recognizing and rewarding the successes in our everyday lives on the way to small and big goals. Because let's be honest, not every day is the same. Some days you may have all the energy in the world. Other days, it's a miracle to get out of bed. Realize that being alive at the end of a tough day is a success in its own right.

#47

Box by Box

Have you ever stood at the base of an actual mountain, stared up, and thought that the top was an impossible distance away? Most goals feel like that too. You get started and suddenly, that great idea you had is big and far away. Your mind reels with this vertigo-inducing panic, "Good-heavens-what-was-I-thinking-I-can't-breathe-kill-me-now." Goals—metaphorical mountains—often feel the same way.

Recently, I moved from Utah to Maryland and I had a literal mountain of boxes to conquer. I'm talking rooms stacked floor to ceiling that could topple over at any moment and bury me so deep in an avalanche of cardboard that it would take rescue crews at least a week to find me. My house made most hoarders look like minimalists. My husband works 11-hour days, including the commute, and my kids are still young enough that when they "help," it triples the work. So the task of unpacking fell to me.

"This is too much," I said. "Clearly the best way to get rid of this mess is to haul it onto the lawn and light a match."

My husband noted that while the kids would enjoy roasting marshmallows, a bonfire was not the best solution.

I laughed at the imagery, but—frustrated and overwhelmed—my chuckles soon turned to tears. In my mind, I was Betsy the Finisher, and I figured I would have the house set up in the space of a week. But I had two book deadlines before the end of summer, and one week turned into two. Two to three. My daughter who is on the autism spectrum grew more anxious by the day; the chaos unsettled her. My other daughter just wanted her doll that was in one of the hundreds of boxes, but who knew which one? Everyone was counting on me and the task before me was so incomprehensible and vast I couldn't see getting it done anymore.

"How am I ever going to do this?" I despaired.

My husband, in his vast wisdom, reminded me what I already knew. "One box at time."

And that was the only way to keep my sanity, by focusing on the one box in front of me. I found a place for everything inside and gave myself a pat on the back when it was empty. Then opened the next one. Repeat.

When the end seems impossibly far away, sometimes you need to put blinders on and focus on putting your foot just one step ahead. One step is easy. Manageable. And so is the next. And the next until you are at the top.

#48

That Finisher's Feeling

You know that warm glow you get when you've done a good job or something hard? That is the rush from finishing, and it's more powerful and potent than a starter's high ever will be. The trick is that most people only think the big stuff matters. Myth. The only way to complete the big stuff is by finishing the small stuff, and I'll tell you a secret: Life is mostly all the small stuff. The seemingly unimportant, everyday, mundane tasks.

Give yourself credit from the little things you do that add up. See success in the small stuff. Instead of being the first to criticize yourself, become the first to offer praise. "Hey, I was really rushing today but I still found time to do that breathing exercise." Hey, some days it's tucking yourself into bed and saying, "I survived."

But if you train yourself to spot your successes, those positive finisher feelings keep you pumped and ready to seek out your next victory. You'll be more active. You'll be more motivated to act on your goal. You'll be far less likely to quit because you'll see the progress you're making through goal keeping. And most important, you'll be fighting that negative voice by building back trust in yourself and adding to that pile of proof that says, Yes, I really can follow through and keep my commitments.

Sometimes you have to sit down for a minute to get a different view of where you stand.

#50

Ta-DONE

It is way too easy to focus on all the things left to do, which is something we are all prone to do when the distance to travel is near equal to how far we've already come. Today, instead of a TO-DO list, write a DONE list. Start from the beginning of your adventure and write out a series of finishes. I'll give you the first few.

> You looked hard at your life and set a goal.
> You committed to that goal and created a plan.

Now it's your turn. Look long and deep. What is different today from when you first opened this book? What is different today from when you hit a particularly low point? How have you grown? What things have you done? Are you happier? Do you feel more organized? Have you been keeping your word to yourself and following through on your action plan? And deeper still, what was something that you did even though you really didn't want to? Sometimes that something is getting out of bed and going to work on a day that feels safer under the covers. Give yourself credit for what you've already achieved on your journey. Focus in on the finisher's feeling and let it propel you to the next task.

Every single journey, no matter how far, is traveled a step at a time.

All it takes is that one step, something everyone can do. Then another. And another. As long as you keep taking those steps, eventually you will always get to the end.

#52

A Goal a Day Keeps the Quitter Away

For me one of the things quitting did was destroy any faith I had in myself to follow through. To commit. To actually stick to things. It took time and daily effort to build that trust back up. Long term was scary. There were all sorts of things waiting out there to jump in my path and knock me off course. So what if I just took it one day at a time?

I started a daily MUST DO list. It usually only had one thing on it, and it varied depending on the day. But I made a promise to myself, that come hell, high water, or puking kids, I would see that one thing done, even if the rest of the day was a total throw away.

So here's what you do, before you go to bed at night: Write a MUST DO for the next day. Write it down so that it confirms the commitment and promise to yourself. It's okay to start small. It doesn't need to be a five-hour task. It can be as simple as getting all the laundry done, running or walking for 45 minutes, or making dinner at home instead of eating out. Then go to sleep. The next day, however, look at your must do. I don't care if the president of the United States drops by to get your opinion on the Middle East—you made a promise and you owe it to yourself to be the kind of friend you deserve. Follow through.

I've totally had those days where not one thing has gone right. On one of these days, I had the unfortunate MUST DO of hitting the gym for 1 hour. Fortunately, I belonged to one of the 24-hour places and my butt was on the elliptical at 11 p.m. It sucked. I was tired. I yawned the entire time. And that is still one of my favorite workout memories because it would have been easier to blow it off—no one would have even known. Except me. And I refused to let myself down anymore.

Keep with one MUST DO a day, and that confidence will grow. It can't be bought at an expensive seminar or retreat. It's something that only you can do by putting in the time.

Procrastination is not a good choice for lazy people.

Because if you put off what needed to be done today, then tomorrow you would have twice as much work to do. Which just sounds exhausting. That's why it's better to put in the time today so that tomorrow will be easier.

#54

The Two-Minute To-Dos

Have you ever noticed that the stuff that gets put off and put off until it builds up to monumental proportions, is crap that only takes two minutes to complete?

One day, I realized that I had put off answering this email for a week. Yet, several times a day during that week, I would remember that I needed to do it and my stomach would cringe. And every day was worse as the pit grew deeper. And the dread lasted longer, never quite leaving my thoughts. That to-do was expensive to keep around, taking space and energy until I got rid of it. Then when I actually did respond, it took less than two minutes. How much of me did I waste? You have to pay rent in your brain for those little procrastinations like not vacuuming, putting away dishes, or paying a bill. I don't know about you, but it gets crowded up there and I'm cheap.

My daughter is much the same way. I try to enforce that if she picks up her clothes for 2 minutes every night, she won't have the hour-long scavenger hunt for socks by the end of the week.

So as a family, we started setting aside 15 minutes a day, an hour before bed, to knock off all the 2-minute to-dos that never managed to get done that day. Then they are off my list, out of my brain, and aren't still racking up data usage when I go to sleep. Not gonna lie, life happens. There are totally days I say screw it, rush the kids to bed, and then grab a roll of cookie dough and crawl under the covers. But honestly, when I wake up the next morning, not only do I have a cookie dough hangover, but I usually stub my toes on the toys left out from the night before.

So the lesson here is a stitch in time saves nine . . . stubbed toes.

#55

Desire and excitement are what get you across the starting line. Daily commitment and consistent effort are what get you across the finish line.

#56

Small deeds done are better than great deeds planned.

—Peter Marshall

#57

There's an App for That

I learned everything I know about rewarding success from when my daughter was in kindergarten. She had a weekly reading chart that we would put on the fridge. And every day she did her 20 minutes, she got a sticker in the date box. And at the end of the week, if she had all her stickers, she got a prize from the teacher's treasure chest.

Just as kids have to learn good habits, there is nothing wrong with a wee bit of bribery when applied correctly. Same holds true for adults. Stickers are not for everyone, but a little motivation and a well-deserved reward is universal. So right now, figure out a reward. Something small that motivates you. Could be a treat. A pair of shoes. An hour to yourself with a good book in a bath. Whatever is a luxury and scarce . . .

Next, figure out a timeframe in which you get your reward. Is it at the end of a week? Or maybe a month?

Then set your task. What do you need to do each day to earn your reward? Maybe it's following through on your MUST DO, your actions set toward your goal, or something completely different and unrelated to your goal. During one of my daughter's rough patches, we made a chart for every day she got through school without crying. (I was having a hard time too, so I did the same.)

Here are a few other examples of what I track:

Days I get up and run

Days I cook dinner versus going out

Days I don't drop a certain four-letter word

You get the picture. You can print off a calendar and hang it up to mark off your completed tasks. You don't have to put an actual gold star—a checkmark will suffice. These days, most phones have fitness tracking or goal apps to help you make notes and see when you've hit the mark and when you've missed. Whatever works for you, mark each day you've complied with your list.

I knew that reward tracking worked for me. But when I watched my daughter experience her success in this very visual way, I saw the way it built her confidence. This sold me on the fact that even adults need to be able to see their progress and not just keep it in their heads.

So make yourself a reward chart. It sounds silly, but the brain needs constant visualization along with various reminders and reinforcements in order to build healthy habits and make changes stick. Below, brainstorm some ideas of things that might be helpful for you to track. Just start writing tasks you do sporadically that you need to increase to turn into a healthy habit. You'll know the right one when you see it.

_____

_____

_____

_____

Act as though everything you do, no matter how small, is just a step that takes you closer to where you want to be.

Every inch closer, no matter how small, matters.

#59

"

Life is like a bicycle. To keep your balance, you must keep moving.

—*Albert Einstein*

"

Swat the Mosquitoes

(Or Other Annoying Naysayers)

THERE WILL ALWAYS BE a few rotten nuts in the peanut gallery. Family, sadly, is not an exception to this rule. Going out of your comfort zone and working toward a goal is scary enough on its own. You already have to fight your own internal critics, heaven knows you don't need more. Ideally, everyone would be on board and cheering you on, but sometimes that is not reality. Some relationships, no matter how much you love a person, can be toxic along the way of reaching your goals. You can't change what other people are gonna do; you can, however, change how you deal with and dodge the crap the monkeys toss at you.

Opinions are like feet—most people have them and sometimes they stink.

Just plug your nose, ignore the smell, keep walking, and move on.

Grit is widely acknowledged as the stuff that separates the quitters from the finishers.

To me it's that little bit of sand an oyster needs to produce a pearl. So if you put these two thoughts together, it just means that in order to get that pearl at the end of the journey, you gotta keep going through the irritating things.

#62

Troll Food

You've probably heard the saying, "Don't feed the trolls," referencing the mean things that people can say online. Let me expand on this: Don't let the trolls under the bridge keep you from crossing it.

After my first book, *Finished Being Fat*, came out, my story was featured in the *Wall Street Journal*. When it hit the online edition, I hurriedly clicked the link and scrolled through the article and picture. I was so proud—until I hit the comments section. People who didn't know me berated my looks, mooing in text at me. They condemned my marriage, making assumptions about my husband. Someone even urged me to kill myself. I couldn't breathe, then I threw up. Fear seized every part of me. And shame. It felt like I'd been physically assaulted. The little voice in the back of my mind, the one I'd worked so hard to shut out, started whispering again. See, you're nothing. You'll never be thin enough. Never be pretty. You aren't worth the oxygen you waste.

Then the *Today* show called my publisher and asked me and my husband to be on the show to share my story as well as to comment on a recent study that stated that being overweight was the number one stressor on a marriage. My publisher was bouncing off the walls to get that kind of exposure for my book. I was hiding under a blanket hoping it would all go away. Nope. No way. No how. I was never going outside again, never mind on national television in front of millions of people. So what if that was my dream? Now it was a nightmare and I wanted no part of it. I'd written my book, achieved my goal. End of story.

My husband is a very private man, and he wasn't exactly dying to share more intimate details of our lives with the masses. However, he knew that this was something I needed to do for my career. I also had a passion for helping people overcome the life of quitting that I narrowly escaped. He encouraged me to do the show and put himself out there in front of everyone with me.

As we prepared to do the segment, I felt naked. How could I help people when I was so afraid to speak? Those 3½ minutes on live television were the longest of my entire life, but I opened myself up and shared my darkest times with the world. The feelings of depression, worthlessness, and all the times I'd tried and quit. Gut clenched, I waited to be objectified, mocked, called out as a phony. The emails started coming within an hour of the show airing. Emails from women sharing their stories with me. Women who had been afraid to speak because they thought they were the only ones who felt broken. I have no illusions about myself. I am only a neurotic lady with more words than sense. But my words were exactly what someone needed to hear. Those 3½ minutes made a difference in someone else's journey. Which wouldn't have happened if I had stayed in my blanket fortress, afraid and hurt because some troll needed to step on me to make themselves feel better.

When you are afraid of putting yourself out there, afraid of ridicule or embarrassment, step back and realize that goals have a ripple effect. And you never know who might be touched or inspired by you.

Everyone has the right to have an opinion, but only you have the power to choose how it effects you.

#64

It doesn't matter if the whole crowd is on their feet cheering—
if one person boos, we will automatically hear the heckler. We
seek approval. It's human nature. But praise is like crack and
criticism like poison. Neither one is very good for me. Instead I
had to realize that my self-esteem wasn't tied to the whims of a
crowd—just to an audience of one. Myself.

#65

Toxic Relationship-like Substances

I absolutely love cinnamon rolls. That does not mean they are good for me. I should really only have them in little portions.

Some people in my life are like cinnamon rolls. I love them, but I should really only be around them in small doses.

Cinnamon rolls don't get me closer to my goals. In fact, they actively hinder my efforts to stay fit. If I ate one every day, I would be a chunky monkey and my health would suffer. When I'm around people (even family) who don't encourage me, or actively hinder me from reaching my goals, my health also suffers. It's just less visible.

In the end, no matter how much I love someone—or baked goods—if it's toxic to me, I owe it to myself and my goals to limit my interaction with them.

#66

For me, when I'm writing or extending myself a bit past my limits, I constantly replay all the things people have said to me, or the things I'm afraid they will say. And considering my books end up on Amazon to be reviewed . . . let's just say those fears can become legion.

So what I've started to do is visualize all the buzzing as gnats whirling around my head. I'll make all the things that bug me, well, into bugs: My well-meaning mother, who thinks I'd be much more successful if I just did _____; my eighth-grade English teacher who claimed I'd never live up to my potential; the bad review that could be waiting in the wings. I'll close my eyes, take a minute to hear what they say—what I'm afraid of—then I picture myself catching each bug in a jar, one by one, and screwing the lid on tight. The bugs are still there, but I can't hear them anymore.

Then I go back to the Why that I've written on the wall. And I repeat it out loud. As I reach for my goal, my voice and my Why are the ones that matter.

#67

What people say is a reflection of them, not you.

    If someone doubts you, it's probably because they themselves would be too afraid to try.

Have faith in yourself, and eventually they will too.

#68

Poo on Pooh

I am a people pleaser by nature. I've always wanted everyone to be happy and like me—as well as the things I did and said. Then I became a writer. The first time I got a one-star review was like a poison-tipped arrow. Something to the effect of, I couldn't get through another page. In real life, this author has to be the most annoying person ever. It sent me into a spiral that paralyzed me and made me rethink every word I typed. I called my agent, Michelle, ranting a mile a minute, listing all the reasons she should drop me as a client.

She gave me the best pep talk ever. Even things universally loved have their haters. Some people don't like chocolate. In fact, there are people who don't like puppies. The horror. Who are these monsters? I refused to believe that they existed, so Michelle had me name my favorite book, something I loved and thought was sheer brilliance. *The Many Adventures of Winnie the Pooh*. This is one of those books that brought so much joy and wonder to my childhood, but as an adult, I'm able to sift through so many layers, go deeper, and find meaning about life, the universe, and everything in between. Not everyone agrees. A quick trip to Goodreads will show you that while most people like or love the book, even that classic has its fair share of critics.

"Winnie the Pooh always seemed a bit weird . . . odd and uncomfortable to my childhood brain, and dull and aimless to my adult one."

"Really. Trust me. It's truly monstrous."

"Am I the only one who hates Winnie the Pooh? I find it torturous. Star for illustrations."

Some even got a bit nasty.

"I love the cartoons, but poor A. A. Milne must've been crazy. I didn't get it at all and there was no way my 6-year-old was going to understand it."

"Had Christopher Robin and his silly old bear been shot in the head at the beginning, it could have been a pretty good book."

I was shocked. Yes, even Winnie the Pooh gets trolled. I felt in my gut that these critiques were clearly written by crazy people, or at least people who read a far different book than I had.

Michelle had made her point though. The fact that someone hated my favorite book didn't alter the fact that I still wholly loved this masterpiece. And while the critic obviously didn't share my excellent taste, I didn't take the trolling personally. And so I should feel the same way about my own books—as long as I did my best and truly believed in them, it shouldn't matter if it's not to someone else's liking.

The same goes for you and your goals. As long as you are doing something you believe in and doing your best, it doesn't matter if someone else thinks it's worthwhile, or if they think you're not what they believe success looks like. Rest assured, they must be one of those crazy people who hate chocolate, puppies, and even Winnie the Pooh.

You are not
a footstool.
Don't let
someone stand
taller by stepping
on your back.

#70

If it wasn't for change, we would have no butterflies. Still, change can be hard to accept and there will always be people who won't let you forget you were once a caterpillar. The best way to prove them wrong is to hop out of that cocoon and soar.

Being doubted by someone doesn't mean that you aren't capable. It only means that some people are incapable of seeing all you can do.

#72

Empowered Empathy

As I said earlier, the most reliable way to change your life is to change how you look at it. Change your perspective, change your reality. That includes how you look at others looking back at you. This is an attitude shift that has served me well, not only in goal reaching, but also in becoming a more compassionate person in general.

I've gotten to the point where I just automatically do this in real time, but in the beginning I would give myself a few minutes each morning.

Start by thinking about someone who has said or done something that has offended you. It can be the jackass that cut you off on the freeway or your mother-in-law's passive/aggressive comment about the pot roast.

Instead of focusing on how their action made you feel, focus on how or why they felt they had to say that. Let's take the road rage guy. I'll come up with a bunch of different scenarios that give him the benefit of the doubt:

> His wife is in labor and he's on the way to the hospital.
> He's got a kid screaming bloody murder in the backseat, so his driving skills are clearly suffering.
> He's really really REALLY got to pee.

Keep doing this, over and over. Let yourself come up with both ridiculous situations as well as deep, heartfelt ones that drive empathy. Once I did this a few times, I went back into my past, looking back at some of the bullying that hurt me so. I imagined situations where they were troubled at home, trying to reach out for help, or inflicting the pain that they felt on others.

After I did that, the pain or offense I felt started to lessen. Instead, I felt bad for them. And then going forward, I didn't always feel on the defense or like I needed to protect myself. What others said didn't affect me as much. Their opinion had become about them and where they were coming from. Not about me.

Scramble to the Summit

(Clawing Your Way to Your Goal)

DOESN'T MATTER WHAT IT IS—the last bit is always the toughest. Whether it's the final cliff, the last 10 pounds, or the last few miles of a marathon, time seems to slow to a crawl and everything is so much harder than it was at first. The end is right there, but no matter how you stretch, it seems out of reach. This is where most turn back defeated. The place that separates the quitters from the finishers.

Bite, claw, and scratch your way to the end. Because the only way to get there is to not stop. You hear me? DON'T STOP. Even if it takes 10 times longer to slog through, you will still be a hundred times better and faster than the folks who turn back.

Success (suc·cess) /sək'ses/

Getting up again to push forward when it's easier to curl up and hide.

#74

Life is an obstacle course. When you hit a wall you have a choice: You can turn back; you can climb over it; or you can grab a sledgehammer and bust through it.

#75

The Road Less Traveled

There are many different ways to get from Point A to Point B. Some folks take the direct path, never looking away from the end. Some take the longer, windier road. Never be ashamed of taking the scenic route. It may take you twice as long, but you'll have experienced twice as much.

When I look back on where I've been and all the wrong turns I've taken and the years spent throwing my energy at things and quitting . . . I'm grateful. I didn't used to be. It used to piss me off. Why, if I had done more productive things earlier, I would be twice as far by now. Maybe I'd even be on the *New York Times* best-sellers list. But then I wouldn't be the person I am now. I wouldn't have every bump, bruise, and scar that made me tougher and stronger and louder with something to say.

Never apologize for taking the road with potholes.

If it was easy,
it wouldn't be
worth it.

Run when you can, walk when you need to, and crawl when that's all you have left.

The most important thing is that you keep moving forward.

#78

> 66
>
> No man ever steps in the same river twice, for it's not the same river and he's not the same man.   —*Heraclitus*
>
> 99

I got this saying in a fortune cookie one day, which on its own is odd since Greek philosophy is not often found at the end of pad thai. It was also odd because it was exactly what I needed to read that day. For weeks I had been trying to run again. Between family medical emergencies, moving, a writing career ... fitness was something that became a luxury and not my goal for that time. Once things settled down, I expected to pick it up easily. Heck, I was a marathon runner. I had the medals and a book to prove it. I laced up my shoes, programmed my watch to alert me after I'd run three miles, set off at a decent pace around the lake behind my house, and promptly found myself wheezing and coughing within 4 minutes, searching for the nearest dang bench to keel over on.

How had I gone from being able to run a half marathon any given weekend to not even making it a quarter mile around the lake? For days, I put off trying again. I was afraid. I wanted to go back to that magical time when everything clicked and I was in the best shape of my life. Days turned into weeks of looking back and chiding myself for not being able to match what I was, what I thought I should be able to be again. My ideal me. Then came the fateful fortune cookie, which ironically was something my yoga teacher would often say to me years ago when I was training for that first race.

It was the reminder I needed that competing against yourself is foolish. One version of yourself will always lose. The same holds true when overcoming past mistakes. You are not the same person—and the circumstances around you aren't the same either. The only possible path is to dip your toes in the water and accept the river for whatever it is right now. Not what it used to be.

#79

My daughter's teacher always tells her,

"A mistake is proof you are trying."

So I figure, bigger mistakes must mean that you were trying something bigger too.

#80

Backpack Meditation

Sometimes the mosquitoes bugging you aren't people at all—just the little niggling stressors of life that nip at us all day. They are stones that weigh us down and make climbing up to our goals that much harder. During my time as a yoga instructor, I would end my classes with this meditation:

Get into a comfortable position. Lay flat on the ground if you can, but just sit quietly if you are in a public or cramped space.

Close your eyes.

Imagine you are hiking through a field of tall grass. You are wearing a backpack. It's so heavy that it wears on your shoulders and bows your back. Imagine you pass by a stream and sit down for a minute. Pull your backpack off your shoulder and set it in front of you. Open the top and you'll see you have been carrying a bag of stones. Each stone represents the stress and the burdens you are carrying. They each have a name etched into it, identifying the stone for what it means. Pull out the top one. Imagine what the burden is and what it says. Is it the fear you have of failure? Or poor body image? Is it the feeling of not being good enough? Or the complexities of work? Take it out and feel the weight of that stone that you carry around. Think long and hard about whether it is worth it to you to lug around. If it's not, toss it into the stream and let it sink to the bottom.

Do this again and again. Pull out a stone; evaluate and weigh it. Some will be gems worth carrying, and others ugly boulders.

Keep what you need and toss the rest. Do this until your pack is empty.

Replace the burdens you need to, close the pack, and hoist it again on your back. Imagine that you can feel the weight and that it is far lighter than before. Elongate your spine without that pressure.

As you start hiking again, your pace is quicker and your gait easier. Cross over a bridge above the stream and get to the other side, leaving your burdens behind.

When you are ready, open your eyes and resume your day.

#81

Case of the Should-Haves

Sometimes at this stage of my goal, I'm stuck with a bunch of "should-have" thoughts. Maybe I went on vacation and missed a week of exercise. Maybe the results weren't quite what I imagined. I should have worked longer and harder. Then I'd have been faster. Or better.

Such thoughts are like running in place. It really just tires me out and doesn't take me anywhere.

Face it—things never look exactly the way we want them to. When I sold my house recently, I got stuck in this should-have rut. I did whatever was humanly possible. The house sold quickly. But then I kept thinking, Well, maybe I should have spiffed up the garden—then it would have sold for more. Or I should have gotten rid of more crap—then I wouldn't have all these boxes to unpack. Unfortunately, houses on the East Coast are twice the cost for half the space.

When I get stuck in those lines of thought, it draws me back to wasting efforts on the roads I didn't take instead of powering through and getting down the road I'm on.

I can't change what I could have done. I can only do as much as I can now.

And reach the finish.

#82

Five-Minute Pity Party

Let's face it. Sometimes things suck. Sometimes life, the universe, and everything else conspire against you and chuck flaming poop bags at your head. If you ignore this fact and smile, act like everything is fine, then some very nice people in white coats are going to haul you off to a padded room.

It's okay to get down sometimes. It's okay to be a bit disappointed. It's not okay to wallow or let it stop you from finishing.

My core group of friends and I have what we like to call the five-minute pity party.

Grab some cookie dough, wine, or just a good friend and set your clock for five minutes.

Hit the timer and let it all out. Whine like a toddler. It's not fair. You did the best you could, but dang the cinnamon roll looked too good. Make excuses. Cry if need be. It is hard. And life isn't fair. And you deserve to vent that. For five minutes. Then when that buzzer goes off, change the narrative. It's hard, but I can do hard things. It's not fair, but that just makes it more satisfying when I make it. I could give up, but I'm better than that.

Now wipe those tears and put your hiking boots back on. You've got a mountain to climb.

#83

Chased Up a Tree

Not only do I write motivational nonfiction, but I also write young adult novels. There's a saying for us writers: "Never be afraid to chase your character up a tree . . . and then set the branches on fire."

When plotting a good story, I have to be mean to my characters. Especially the ones I like. Why? Because if I don't give them challenges and tough patches and throw everything I have at them, they won't grow to be a strong enough hero to triumph in the end.

So as this part gets harder, and stuff feels stacked against you, think of it within the same terms. They are only challenges put there to make you strong enough to be the hero of your own story.

When you feel like quitting, when the finish line is not worth the struggle ... think about why you started to begin with.

#85

Countdown to the Finish

It's a trick parents have used for ages to pass the time as Christmas draws near. Countdown to the big finish.

So if I have 30 days left in my goal statement, instead of continuing toward the thing linearly, I would reverse it and start counting backward. The number left to go continually grows smaller. It's a little bit of a brain psych but it totally works. It reminds us that today we're closer to the goal than yesterday. And tomorrow will be closer still.

And as you get closer, work on visualizing what your life looks like with your goal fulfilled.

You had a strong Why. A need. So as you achieve that need, picture yourself crossing that line and getting what you've been working so hard for. Picture like it is going to happen in the next minute. And keep that mental image in your mind as you slog through the end. Get excited for the finisher's rush, and let the adrenaline do some of the work for you.

You are almost there. And getting closer. And closer . . .

Keep going when the end is in sight—otherwise you will never know what is on the other side.

#87

"

The difference between winning and losing is most often not quitting.

—*Walt Disney*

"

#88

Attitude of Gratitude

You can't be miserable and grateful at the same time. It's impossible. So when I am stuck on those last few miles of a race, or the last few chapters of a book, or the last dozen boxes—and I am just so done I never want to see another piece of cardboard for the rest of my life—I try to find an attitude of gratitude. I look back on where I've been on this journey and how far I've come. Then I'll journal some of the sticky parts that were hard to get over, and then detail how I got over them. And who helped me. Then I'll write them a letter. Sometimes I'll send them; other times it's to a person I just happened to cross paths with and will never see again, but that meeting changed things or was significant for me. So I'll write them a letter in my journal as if they would read it.

The exercise is simple, and it goes like this:

Below, write three things that have gone very well on your goal journey.

Next, write three things that you struggle with, but overcame. How did you get past those things?

_____
_____
_____

Next, write three things or people that made a difference and helped along the way. It can be something you read. The bartender you sobbed to that encouraged you to keep going. Your spouse for watching the kids while you ran to the gym. But find three.

_____
_____
_____

Last, write at least one of those three people or things (yes even if it was an event or object) a heartfelt letter that expresses your gratitude and explains how their actions helped you.

_____
_____
_____

You don't have to give it to that person. But I can tell you that oftentimes they don't know that they matter. And maybe they need to hear that too.

Enjoy the View

(Without Falling Off the Cliff)

EVEN WHEN YOU'VE CLIMBED A MOUNTAIN and relished the view from the top, the work is not over. You still have to climb down. It's far too easy to stand at the summit and, instead of enjoying the view, peer over at a taller mountain and wish you'd taken that route instead.

But you can't go back and once you've tasted that finisher's rush, the tendency is to try to leap from peak to peak like a mountain goat. If you tackle your entire goal list all at once, it's inevitable to become burdened and start the quitting cycle all over again. Don't take on too much. You can't do all of it and expect to succeed at each one. There's not enough time or energy.

Instead, cement the changes you've made and avoid burning out by using these last thoughts to prioritize and accept whatever level you're at.

#89

Where's My Parade

Congratulations! You did it. You reached your goal. Now what?

I remember being at the top of a literal mountain and it was the hardest thing I had ever done, and I wanted there to be a ticker tape parade, complete with a band and confetti and a throng of people all applauding what I had done. Where was my marching band, gold medal, and giant check or plaque for the wall? And worse than that, it occurred to me that I still had to climb down the mountain.

Not all goals are public and obvious to those outside. Some are deeply personal and only you might realize the extent of the change. Beyond that, after such a huge life event, something highly anticipated, there is always the downhill. Like waiting all year for Christmas, and then finding yourself on December 26. Now what?

I had to take time to build my own parade and find ways that were meaningful to me to celebrate my accomplishments. Whether it was a book-launch party or a shopping trip for a smaller size. Then I'd pass it on. Share what I'd learned with someone else.

That's what helps me get past the post-goal comedown.

#90

The Shiny Finisher's Medal

I will be completely honest. There are three reasons I run. One, it's hard and I hate every second of it. But I like to prove I can do it anyway. Two, if I run enough miles, I can eat a cinnamon roll. And three, when I run races, they give me a sparkly medal at the finish line.

I love those medals. I hang them on my wall and they remind me that even though I used to have trouble running one block, I can now run 13 or 26 miles. In a row. It's the unthinkable for a former sloth like me.

I said before that quitting built a wall of failures. And how do you get over it? By building a mountain of finishes. For me at least, I find it helpful to have something I can see. Something I can hold in my hands that represents what I've done. Not all goals are races that have actual finish lines with shiny trinkets at the end. But every goal has a finisher's medal—you just have to know how to find it.

I would love to tell you to detail out exactly the method of finding your medal . . . but I can't. It's something deeply personal that will have meaning when you see it. I know—big help, right? Isn't this supposed to be instructive?

Well, I can only tell you that you need to find them. And give you a few examples I keep around:

After I lost weight, I had very nice family pictures taken. I keep some framed in my office.

The broken music box is proof I survived my move, despite the difficulties.

I have a lotus blossom tattooed on my wrist to commemorate 10 years since depression had me low enough to consider suicide.

I keep a stack of all my rejection letters from agents before my books started getting published.

I have the shoes with holes in them after I ran my first 500 miles.

Here are some other examples:

Maybe if you quit smoking, a Ziploc bag with a pile of ashes.

A certificate of completion.

A picture.

A part of the outfit you wore when you hit your peak.

Keep your medals safe in a box or on a shelf and look at them often and remember that whatever you were, now you are a finisher.

Once you've
done one
thing that
was impossible,
suddenly
EVERYTHING
is possible.

#92

Hindsight Sucks

Well, it's true. The funny thing about looking down is that the road you took looks a hell of a lot smaller and you can see every little zig and zag you took. There is a tendency to stand up there and deconstruct the route, finding the faults to be better and faster the next time.

I fight this urge all the time. Often I fight to be happy and take the same approach I do with my running. At the end of the race, as I'm hobbling after the finish line, I think back to the times I had to walk. Or that my time was slower than my last race. Instead, I focus on that medal and a single thought:

I am grateful that I can run at all.

It is impossible to be wistful, covetous, and grateful at the same time. By amping up that gratitude for everything I fought for that may not have been perfect, I can truly appreciate that they were mine. And by God I can just be happy where I am and not still be stuck in quitter's hell.

#93

Balancing Act

As my pile of finishes got bigger, the fiery glow of finishing made that old starting high look like a flashlight.

I wanted more. I had the brilliant idea that I could make up for years of quitting by doing 10 times as much as any sane person. Because hey, I was a finisher. I wrote a book. I was on the *Today* show. Al Roker had called my husband a jerk . . . I could get through anything.

Bzzt. Wrong.

Now that I was fit and skinny, I decided I needed to keep that up—with three-hour sessions at the gym. And hey my writing career was booming and along with *Finished Being Fat*, my fiction book *Spelled* got picked up. And they wanted to sign it up as a trilogy. So write two more books. No problem. But I also got certified in yoga, so sure I could teach community classes once a week. And then travel with a color 5K every few months. And coach a kid's creative problem-solving group. And volunteer on the PTA . . .

For being a yoga instructor, my balance sucked. As you might imagine, I fell flat on my face. It wasn't possible to do all of those things, to give each one my full focus. If all of me is 100 percent, at best each task got 20 percent of my attention. My family never saw me and soon I had trouble seeing myself. I was Betsy, The Finisher. I couldn't quit. I agreed to do all these things . . .

I nearly burnt myself out. I wasn't sleeping. Barely eating. Just trying to meet all my obligations. Eventually my husband sat me down for a come-to-Jesus talk. I was not only burning the candle at both ends, but had a flame under the middle as well. He helped me go through my list and trim down the obligations that could wait for a season, and push forward on the ones with a tighter deadline.

I still have trouble saying no but I have realized that I still have goals and dreams. And each one deserves more than a 20 percent hobble up the mountain. What I learned most is that I have an obligation to take care of myself, to make sure I keep myself in tip-top shape—mentally, physically, and emotionally. Then I can give to others and race up more mountains.

Little goals reached are worth far more than big goals written down on a bucket list.

#95

Pride and Priorities

In the world of to-dos, there's an endless list. You can't do them all at once. And some of them seem important now, but when weighed against other things, really aren't.

Stephen Covey has a four-quadrant system that works better for business folks. I have a quadrant system for the rest of us.

First, write down all the things you need to do, the goals you want to go after or the things you feel you need to maintain. I will put examples from mine here:

Maintain waist size
Maintain fitness
Volunteer for kids Halloween party at school
Book signings
Learn to knit
Learn to cook
Write third book in series
Stop drinking soda
Finish degree

Then I make this chart thing:

Pride	Quality of Life

Time Sensitive	Need

Then I start looking at each of those to-dos and weigh why I should do them. Do I want to keep my figure for vanity? At this point, mostly. As long as I'm healthy . . . I don't need three hours obsessing in the gym. So I'd shove that to pride. Learn to cook? Well, my family would appreciate it. So that would improve quality of life and is a point of pride, but is not needed or time sensitive. So I'd add it in both those quadrants. Book three is time sensitive and under contract, so needed.

After I've plugged everything in, I look at my quadrant and first pluck out the ones labeled Need and Time Sensitive. Then I'll look through the quadrants Time Sensitive and Quality of Life. For those, I will have to ask myself if the benefit is worth the time it is going to cost me. Then I go back to the rest of the Need quadrant. Then the Quality of Life. The last is Pride.

Realistically I can usually only devote my energies to four or five things at once. So I rarely get any non–time-sensitive things. Right now. But life changes. And so do the lists. So it's good to do this exercise regularly to see what's important right now. And put the other things on a shelf for later. The mountains are there . . . but they can wait for another day to be climbed.

The view from the top of the mountain is always pretty.

But looking back down and knowing you slogged through the swamps in the valleys and scaled the cliffs by the end of your fingernails—that's what changes the view from beautiful to breathtaking.

#97

The to-do list is not a to-do novel. As you move on from one goal to the next, keep it small.

Keep it focused. Don't prioritize your schedule to find time to do it all.

Schedule your priorities and then you will be able to do them all in time.

#98

The journey was long. And I'm guessing that parts were tough. But you have something that you will always be able to say to yourself with confidence now:

"Sure it's hard, but I can do hard things."

#99

Rivers know this: there is no hurry. We shall get there some day.

—*A. A. Milne*

Your path is set. You are changing, you are finishing. Celebrate each goal and each success for what it is without rushing to complete the next one. You'll get there—there's no big hurry. Enjoy the peace in trusting yourself and knowing you can and will reach your goals without that stress of "right now."

#100

The Endless Summit

There will always be more goals. More metaphoric mountains to climb, but if you've truly changed your perspective, that is one you never have to climb again. The mountain of finishes that towers over the wall built from quitting. And by living the Philosophy of Finishing, you are always standing at the peak. The summit is endless—it just keeps getting bigger the more you add to that pile.

That little voice has no power over you anymore because you can prove it's full of crap and that it's lying. You can do hard things, see. Here are the finisher's medals to prove it.

And as you look out from the finisher's peak you know that, with commitment, passion, and effort, you really can go after anything that you really wanted. You know how to use your Why to drive you forward past the vultures that tell you no.

Be yourself, whoever it is you choose to become. It's yours for the taking.

Go get it.

ABOUT THE AUTHOR

Betsy Schow and her Philosophy of Finishing have been featured on *The Today Show*, NPR, the *Wall St. Journal* and more. She's teaches the power of self-reliance and goal reaching through both her non-fiction motivational works and her young adult fantasy books, The Storymakers series: *Spelled* and *Wanted*. Currently she lives with her family on a lake in Baltimore, where she runs, writes, and reinvents the wheel teaching kids creative problem solving with Odyssey of the Mind.

You can contact to her through her website, betsyschow.com.